Gratitude, Every Day

Gratitude, Every Day

365 Daily Affirmations to Step Into the Life You Were Meant to Live

Christine Zanjanipour

ISBN: 979-8-9939013-9-8

First Edition

Published by Details Matter Books

Printed in the United States of America

For Tracy, my best friend.

Pure joy, pure light, pure love. Thank you for being exactly who you are. Every room is brighter because of you.

&

Introduction

There was a time in my life when I believed gratitude was something you felt only after everything was going right.

After the breakthrough.

After the healing.

After the answers arrived.

After life finally looked the way you hoped it would.

But over time, I began to understand something far more powerful.

Gratitude is not a reward for a perfect life.

It is the doorway into one.

The moments that transformed me most were not always the biggest moments. Often, they were the quiet ones.

A sunrise over the mountains.

A deep breath after a difficult season.

The sound of water nearby.

A conversation that reminded me I was not alone.

The realization that even in uncertain moments, there was still beauty to be found.

Gratitude changed the way I saw my life.

Not because everything suddenly became easy, but because I began paying attention differently.

I began noticing what was already here.

What was already beautiful.

What was already enough.

And slowly, life began to feel softer.

Calmer.

Richer.

More meaningful.

This book was created to help you experience that shift for yourself.

Not through pressure or perfection, but through small daily moments of awareness and appreciation.

Some days, the words in these pages may simply bring you peace.

Other days, they may help you reconnect with yourself in a deeper way.

And maybe, over time, they will help you realize something important:

The life you are searching for is not as far away as you think.

Sometimes the shift begins with a single moment of gratitude.

My hope is that this book becomes part of your daily rhythm.

A place you return to in the morning before the world gets loud.

A reminder to slow down, breathe deeply, and notice the beauty that still exists around you.

You do not need to have everything figured out.

You do not need to feel grateful every second of every day.

You simply need to begin noticing.

One moment.

One breath.

One page at a time.

Thank you for allowing this book to become part of your journey.

How to Use This Book

There is no right or wrong way to experience this book.

You may choose to begin with Day 1 and move through each page slowly, allowing gratitude to become part of your daily rhythm.

Or, you may use this book intuitively.

Hold it close to your heart, take a deep breath, and quietly say:

"Today, I allow the universe to show me what I need to know."

Then open the book to any page and trust that the words waiting for you are exactly what you were meant to receive in that moment.

Some days, a single sentence may stay with you.

Other days, an affirmation may shift your entire perspective.

Do not rush through these pages.

Pause.

Reflect.

Return often.

This book is not meant to be completed.

It is meant to be experienced.

Trust the page you land on.

Love,
Christine

Day 1

Gratitude turns what you have into more than enough.

❧

Today, I begin with gratitude.
I honor where I am, knowing it is enough, and
from here, everything expands.

Day 2

What you appreciate, appreciates.

I notice the good in my life, and as I do, more good reveals itself to me.

Day 3

Gratitude shifts everything.

&

Even the smallest moments hold beauty.
Today, I choose to see it.

Day 4

There is always something to be thankful for.

❧

I train my mind to find what is working.
My life responds in kind.

DAY 5

Gratitude is a perspective.

I see my life through the lens of appreciation.
Everything feels lighter because of it.

Day 6

Simple things become extraordinary when you notice them.

❧

I am grateful for the quiet, the calm, and the ordinary moments that shape my life.

Day 7

Gratitude begins where comparison ends.

I release comparison.
My journey is mine, and I am thankful for it.

Day 8

Gratitude brings you back to yourself.

❧

I return to the present moment with appreciation.
This is where my power lives.

Day 9

Enough is a decision.

I decide that my life is enough today.
And in that decision, I feel peace.

Day 10

Gratitude is grounding.

❧

No matter what is happening around me, I anchor into gratitude.

Day 11

The more you thank life, the more life gives you to thank.

❧

Gratitude expands my reality in ways I cannot yet see.

DAY 12

Gratitude is magnetic.

I attract more to be grateful for simply by appreciating what already is.

DAY 13

Thankfulness is abundance.

❧

I live in abundance because I recognize it everywhere.

Day 14

Gratitude multiplies joy.

❧

Joy grows in my life as I acknowledge it.

Day 15

Energy flows where attention goes.

I place my attention on what is good, and it grows.

Day 16

Gratitude opens doors.

❧

Opportunities flow to me because I appreciate what I already have.

Day 17

Life responds to appreciation.

I feel supported, guided, and deeply grateful.

Day 18

Gratitude is trust in disguise.

❧

I trust that everything unfolding is working for me.

DAY 19

Thankfulness creates momentum.

❧

My gratitude propels me forward in powerful ways.

Day 20

Gratitude changes the story.

I rewrite my story through appreciation.

Day 21

Gratitude is who you become.

&

I am a grateful person.
It is part of my identity.

Day 22

You do not practice gratitude, you live it.

❧

Gratitude flows through me naturally and effortlessly.

Day 23

Gratitude is a way of being.

I embody appreciation in everything I do.

Day 24

Gratitude is power.

❧

My gratitude elevates my energy and my life.

DAY 25

You become what you focus on.

❧

I become more fulfilled as I focus on what I love.

Day 26

Gratitude is presence.

❧

I am fully present, and deeply thankful for this moment.

Day 27

Gratitude is awareness.

I see the beauty in places I once overlooked.

Day 28

Gratitude is expansion.

My life continues to expand as I remain grateful.

Day 29

Gratitude is alignment.

❧

I feel aligned, supported, and at peace.

DAY 30

Gratitude is the beginning of everything.

❧

Everything I desire begins with appreciation, and I have already begun.

Day 31

Gratitude begins where resistance ends.

Today, I release the need to resist what is. I soften into acceptance, and I find gratitude waiting for me there.

Day 32

There is beauty in simply being.

❧

I do not need to rush or prove anything.
I am grateful for this moment, exactly as it is.

Day 33

Gratitude lives in the present moment.

I bring my awareness back to now.
Here, in this moment, there is so much to appreciate.

Day 34

Small moments hold great meaning.

❧

I notice the quiet details of my life.
They are filled with more beauty than I once realized.

Day 35

Gratitude softens everything.

What once felt heavy begins to feel lighter.
I allow gratitude to gently shift my perspective.

Day 36

Gratitude is a choice you make again and again.

❧

Today, I choose gratitude, even in the smallest ways.
Each choice brings more peace into my life.

Day 37

There is always something working for you.

Even when I cannot see it, I trust that things are unfolding in my favor.
I am grateful for what is happening behind the scenes.

Day 38

Gratitude creates space for peace.

❧

I release tension and welcome calm into my life. Gratitude opens the door to a deeper sense of peace.

Day 39

You are allowed to slow down.

I give myself permission to pause.
In slowing down, I find more to be grateful for.

Day 40

Gratitude is grounding.

❧

No matter what is happening around me, I return to what is steady and good.
I am supported, I am safe, I am grateful.

Day 41

Gratitude invites more of what you love.

I focus on what brings me joy.
As I do, more of it flows into my life.

Day 42

Gratitude is abundance in its simplest form.

I recognize the fullness already present in my life.
I am surrounded by abundance.

Day 43

What you notice grows.

❧

I choose to notice the good.
My life reflects that choice back to me.

Day 44

Gratitude changes how you see everything.

❧

I look at my life through a lens of appreciation.
Everything begins to feel different.

Day 45

There is magic in appreciation.

❧

The more I appreciate, the more life surprises me.
I am open to that magic.

Day 46

Gratitude is a quiet kind of power.

❧

I do not need to force or chase.
My gratitude draws good things toward me naturally.

Day 47

You are already living moments you once wished for.

I pause and recognize how far I have come.
I am grateful for the life I am living today.

Day 48

Gratitude strengthens trust.

❧

The more I appreciate, the more I trust the path I am on.
Everything is leading me somewhere meaningful.

DAY 49

Gratitude opens your heart.

❧

I allow myself to feel deeply grateful. My heart expands with every moment of appreciation.

DAY 50

Gratitude connects you to what matters.

❧

I focus on what truly matters in my life.
I am grateful for what fills my heart.

Day 51

Gratitude becomes who you are.

Gratitude is not something I do, it is part of who I am.
I carry it with me everywhere I go.

Day 52

You can return to gratitude at any time.

❧

No matter what I am feeling, I can shift.
Gratitude is always available to me.

Day 53

Gratitude brings you back to center.

When I feel scattered, I return to appreciation. It grounds me and brings me back to myself.

Day 54

Gratitude is clarity.

I see my life more clearly through gratitude.
What matters becomes obvious to me.

Day 55

Gratitude creates calm within you.

I breathe in peace and exhale tension.
Gratitude settles my mind and body.

Day 56

Gratitude is a steady presence.

❧

Even as life changes, gratitude remains constant within me.
It is something I can always return to.

Day 57

Gratitude helps you receive.

❧

I open myself to receiving more goodness in my life.
I am worthy of all that is coming to me.

Day 58

Gratitude is alignment.

I feel aligned with who I am becoming.
Gratitude brings me into harmony with my life.

Day 59

Gratitude is expansion.

My life continues to expand as I remain grateful.
There is always more waiting for me.

DAY 60

Gratitude is the foundation.

Everything I am building begins with appreciation. I am grateful for what is, and excited for what is to come.

DAY 61

Gratitude deepens your awareness.

❧

I notice more of what is good in my life.
With awareness, my gratitude continues to grow.

Day 62

There is richness in the present moment.

I slow down and fully experience my life.
This moment holds more than enough.

Day 63

Gratitude brings clarity to your path.

As I appreciate where I am, my next steps become clear.
I trust the direction of my life.

Day 64

Gratitude transforms the ordinary.

❧

What once felt routine now feels meaningful.
I see beauty in the everyday moments of my life.

Day 65

Gratitude invites calm into your mind.

I release overthinking and return to appreciation. My mind becomes quiet and at ease.

Day 66

Gratitude is a gentle shift.

&

I do not force change, I allow it.
Gratitude naturally moves me into a better place.

Day 67

Gratitude connects you to joy.

❧

Joy is always available to me.
I access it through appreciation.

Day 68

Gratitude softens your perspective.

❧

I choose to see my life with kindness and understanding.
Everything feels lighter because of it.

Day 69

Gratitude brings you back to what matters.

I focus on what truly matters in my life.
Everything else begins to fade.

Day 70

Gratitude creates inner peace.

❧

I feel a deep sense of calm within me.
Peace grows as I continue to appreciate my life.

Day 71

Gratitude is a daily return.

❧

No matter where my mind goes, I return to gratitude.
It is always here for me.

Day 72

Gratitude expands your perspective.

❧

I see beyond limitations and into possibility.
My life feels bigger and more open.

Day 73

Gratitude is presence.

I am fully here, fully aware, and fully grateful.
This moment is enough.

Day 74

Gratitude creates space for possibility.

❧

As I appreciate what is, I open myself to what could be.
My life is full of possibility.

Day 75

Gratitude brings ease.

❧

I release the need to struggle.
I allow life to feel easier and more supportive.

Day 76

Gratitude is a powerful habit.

Each day, I strengthen my practice of appreciation.
It becomes more natural to me.

Day 77

Gratitude is a way of seeing.

I choose to see my life through a grateful lens.
Everything shifts because of it.

Day 78

Gratitude is quiet strength.

&

I feel grounded and strong in my appreciation.
It supports me in every moment.

Day 79

Gratitude reveals what is already working.

❧

I focus on what is going well in my life.
There is more working than I once realized.

Day 80

Gratitude creates momentum.

❧

Each moment of appreciation builds on the next. My life continues to move forward in a positive way.

DAY 81

Gratitude connects you to yourself.

I feel deeply connected to who I am.
Gratitude brings me home to myself.

Day 82

Gratitude is a steady foundation.

❧

No matter what changes, I remain grounded in appreciation.
It supports me through everything.

Day 83

Gratitude shifts your energy.

I feel my energy lift as I focus on the good.
Everything begins to feel different.

Day 84

Gratitude opens new perspectives.

❧

I am open to seeing my life in new ways.
There is always more to discover.

DAY 85

Gratitude invites ease into your day.

I move through my day with calm and appreciation.
Everything flows more easily.

Day 86

Gratitude builds trust within you.

❧

I trust myself and my path.
Gratitude strengthens that trust.

Day 87

Gratitude is a quiet anchor.

❧

When things feel uncertain, I return to appreciation.
It steadies me.

Day 88

Gratitude creates balance.

❧

I hold space for both growth and appreciation.
My life feels balanced and whole.

Day 89

Gratitude is expansion in motion.

❧

As I remain grateful, my life continues to expand.
I welcome all that is unfolding.

Day 90

Gratitude is a new beginning.

&

Each day, I begin again with appreciation.
Every moment is a fresh start.

Day 91

Gratitude is a quiet beginning.

I begin today with appreciation.
It sets the tone for everything that follows.

Day 92

Gratitude brings light to your day.

❧

I notice what feels good and let it brighten my life. Lightness flows through me.

Day 93

Gratitude is a gentle reminder.

I remember all that is already good.
I do not overlook the blessings in my life.

Day 94

Gratitude is awareness in action.

❧

I actively notice what I appreciate.
My awareness deepens with every moment.

Day 95

Gratitude creates openness.

I open myself to new experiences and perspectives.
Gratitude keeps me receptive and present.

Day 96

Gratitude is a calming force.

❧

I feel calm and centered as I focus on appreciation.
Peace moves through me effortlessly.

Day 97

Gratitude invites alignment.

❧

I feel aligned with my life and my path.
Everything is coming together for me.

Day 98

Gratitude is a steady presence.

No matter what changes, gratitude remains within me.
It is always available to me.

Day 99

Gratitude brings clarity to your heart.

I understand what matters most to me.
Gratitude helps me feel it clearly.

Day 100

Gratitude marks a milestone.

I celebrate how far I have come.
I am proud of the life I am creating.

Day 101

Gratitude is appreciation in its purest form.

❧

I feel genuine appreciation for my life.
Nothing needs to change for me to feel grateful.

Day 102

Gratitude connects you to abundance.

❧

I see abundance all around me.
I am surrounded by more than enough.

Day 103

Gratitude softens expectations.

I release the need for things to be perfect.
I appreciate what is here now.

Day 104

Gratitude is a grounding force.

❧

I feel steady and supported.
Gratitude keeps me rooted in the present.

Day 105

Gratitude invites trust.

I trust the process of my life.
Everything is unfolding as it should.

Day 106

Gratitude is expansion from within.

❧

My inner world expands with appreciation.
My outer world follows.

Day 107

Gratitude is a quiet confidence.

I feel confident in where I am.
Gratitude reminds me that I am on the right path.

DAY 108

Gratitude creates connection.

❧

I feel connected to my life and the people in it. Appreciation deepens my relationships.

Day 109

Gratitude brings perspective.

❧

I see my life more clearly.
There is more good than I once realized.

Day 110

Gratitude is a gentle guide.

❧

I let gratitude lead my thoughts and actions. It guides me in the right direction.

Day 111

Gratitude is presence in motion.

❧

I stay present as I move through my day.
Every moment holds something to appreciate.

Day 112

Gratitude is a soft landing.

❧

No matter how my day unfolds, I return to appreciation.
It brings me back to peace.

Day 113

Gratitude reveals what matters.

I focus on what truly matters in my life.
Everything else fades away.

Day 114

Gratitude creates space for joy.

❧

I allow joy to enter my life.
Gratitude makes room for it.

Day 115

Gratitude is a daily practice.

❧

I show up for this practice each day.
It becomes a natural part of who I am.

Day 116

Gratitude builds resilience.

❧

I move through challenges with appreciation.
It strengthens me from within.

Day 117

Gratitude is a gentle reset.

I pause and shift my perspective.
Gratitude brings me back to center.

Day 118

Gratitude invites flow.

❧

I allow my life to flow with ease.
Appreciation keeps me open and aligned.

Day 119

Gratitude is a steady rhythm.

I move through life with a sense of balance.
Gratitude keeps me grounded and steady.

Day 120

Gratitude creates harmony.

I feel harmony within myself and my life.
Everything feels more aligned.

Day 121

Gratitude is a quiet celebration.

❧

I celebrate the small and meaningful moments.
They are what make life beautiful.

Day 122

Gratitude is a deeper awareness.

❧

I see beyond the surface of my life.
There is so much more to appreciate.

Day 123

Gratitude invites presence.

❧

I am fully here in this moment.
This moment is enough.

Day 124

Gratitude brings softness.

❧

I approach my life with gentleness and care.
Gratitude softens my experience.

Day 125

Gratitude is a steady light.

❧

Even in uncertainty, I find something to appreciate.
That light guides me forward.

Day 126

Gratitude opens your perspective.

&

I see new possibilities in my life.
Gratitude expands my view.

DAY 127

Gratitude is a quiet strength.

I feel strong and grounded in appreciation.
It supports me through everything.

Day 128

Gratitude creates ease.

❧

I release tension and welcome ease.
Life flows more naturally for me.

Day 129

Gratitude is a return to self.

❧

I come back to who I am through appreciation.
I feel centered and whole.

Day 130

Gratitude is awareness of the good.

❧

I focus on what is going well.
There is always something to appreciate.

Day 131

Gratitude builds inner peace.

I feel peaceful and calm within.
Gratitude deepens that feeling.

Day 132

Gratitude is a conscious choice.

I choose appreciation again and again.
It shapes my experience of life.

DAY 133

Gratitude invites clarity.

My mind feels clear and focused.
Gratitude brings me that clarity.

Day 134

Gratitude is a steady anchor.

❧

No matter what is happening, I remain grounded.
Gratitude anchors me.

Day 135

Gratitude opens the heart.

I allow myself to feel deeply.
Gratitude expands my heart.

Day 136

Gratitude creates presence.

I am fully engaged in my life.
Each moment matters to me.

Day 137

Gratitude invites trust in yourself.

❧

I trust my decisions and my path.
Gratitude strengthens that trust.

DAY 138

Gratitude is a gentle awareness.

I move through my day with quiet appreciation.
It stays with me.

Day 139

Gratitude creates a sense of enough.

I feel content with where I am.
There is nothing missing in this moment.

Day 140

Gratitude invites calm.

❧

I feel calm and steady.
Gratitude brings me peace.

Day 141

Gratitude is a steady flow.

&

Appreciation flows through me naturally.
It becomes effortless.

Day 142

Gratitude brings you back to balance.

❧

I feel balanced and grounded.
Gratitude centers me.

Day 143

Gratitude invites expansion.

❧

I open myself to growth and possibility.
My life continues to expand.

Day 144

Gratitude is a quiet knowing.

❧

I know that everything is working out for me.
Gratitude deepens that belief.

Day 145

Gratitude is a peaceful presence.

I feel peaceful in my life.
Gratitude supports that feeling.

Day 146

Gratitude creates awareness of joy.

❧

I notice moments of joy throughout my day.
They are always there.

Day 147

Gratitude invites ease and flow.

I allow my life to feel lighter.
Everything flows with more ease.

Day 148

Gratitude is a quiet transformation.

❧

Change happens naturally within me.
Gratitude is leading that change.

DAY 149

Gratitude is a deeper connection.

I feel connected to my life and my purpose.
Gratitude strengthens that connection.

Day 150

Gratitude is the path forward.

❧

I move forward with appreciation and trust.
Everything is unfolding beautifully.

Day 151

Gratitude is a fresh perspective.

I see my life through new eyes.
Everything feels more meaningful to me.

Day 152

Gratitude invites lightness.

❧

I release heaviness and welcome ease.
My life feels lighter today.

Day 153

Gratitude is a daily renewal.

&

Each day, I begin again with appreciation.
I am always starting fresh.

Day 154

Gratitude deepens your experience.

❧

I feel my life more fully.
Gratitude brings depth to every moment.

Day 155

Gratitude is awareness of beauty.

I notice beauty all around me.
It has always been here.

Day 156

Gratitude invites calm energy.

My energy feels steady and peaceful.
I move through my day with ease.

Day 157

Gratitude is a quiet confidence.

I trust where I am in life.
Everything is unfolding in the right way.

Day 158

Gratitude connects you to peace.

❧

I feel peaceful within myself.
Gratitude brings me back to that place.

Day 159

Gratitude reveals simplicity.

&

Life does not need to be complicated.
I appreciate the simplicity of this moment.

Day 160

Gratitude is a steady guide.

I allow appreciation to guide my thoughts.
It leads me in the right direction.

DAY 161

Gratitude brings clarity of mind.

❧

My thoughts feel clear and focused.
Gratitude creates that clarity.

Day 162

Gratitude invites trust in life.

I trust the unfolding of my life.
Everything is working in my favor.

Day 163

Gratitude creates emotional ease.

❧

I feel calm within my emotions.
Gratitude softens everything I feel.

Day 164

Gratitude is a grounding force.

I feel stable and supported.
Gratitude keeps me grounded.

Day 165

Gratitude opens new doors.

&

I am open to new opportunities.
Gratitude leads me to them.

DAY 166

Gratitude is a steady rhythm.

❧

I move through my day with calm consistency.
Gratitude keeps me centered.

Day 167

Gratitude invites presence in every moment.

❧

I stay present in what I am doing.
Each moment matters.

Day 168

Gratitude reveals what is working.

❧

I focus on what is going well.
There is more working than I realized.

Day 169

Gratitude is a quiet awareness.

❧

I move through my day with gentle appreciation.
It stays with me.

Day 170

Gratitude invites harmony.

❧

I feel balanced and aligned.
My life flows in harmony.

Day 171

Gratitude is a peaceful choice.

I choose peace through appreciation.
It changes how I feel.

Day 172

Gratitude expands your heart.

❧

My heart feels open and full.
Gratitude expands my capacity to feel.

Day 173

Gratitude is a gentle reminder of enough.

I have enough.
I am enough.
This moment is enough.

Day 174

Gratitude invites calm thinking.

❧

My mind feels quiet and steady.
Gratitude clears my thoughts.

Day 175

Gratitude creates a sense of fulfillment.

&

I feel fulfilled in my life.
Gratitude brings that feeling to me.

Day 176

Gratitude is a steady presence.

❧

Even as things change, gratitude remains.
It is always within me.

Day 177

Gratitude builds inner strength.

I feel strong and supported.
Gratitude strengthens me from within.

Day 178

Gratitude invites ease into your life.

❧

I allow my life to feel easier.
Everything flows naturally.

Day 179

Gratitude reveals quiet joy.

I notice moments of joy throughout my day.
They are always present.

Day 180

Gratitude is a turning point.

I shift my focus to appreciation.
Everything begins to change.

Day 181

Gratitude is a calm awareness.

❧

I feel aware and present.
Gratitude keeps me centered.

Day 182

Gratitude invites trust in yourself.

❧

I trust my choices and my path.
Gratitude reinforces that trust.

DAY 183

Gratitude creates balance within you.

I feel balanced in my thoughts and emotions.
Gratitude brings me back to center.

Day 184

Gratitude is a quiet expansion.

❧

My life continues to grow.
Gratitude supports that expansion.

Day 185

Gratitude invites clarity in your life.

I see my path more clearly.
Gratitude brings that clarity.

Day 186

Gratitude is a steady connection.

I feel connected to my life and purpose.
Gratitude strengthens that connection.

DAY 187

Gratitude creates a peaceful state.

I feel calm and at ease.
Gratitude brings me into peace.

Day 188

Gratitude invites openness.

❧

I am open to new experiences.
Gratitude keeps me receptive.

Day 189

Gratitude is a gentle perspective.

I see my life with kindness.
Everything feels softer.

DAY 190

Gratitude creates a sense of flow.

❧

My life flows with ease.
Gratitude keeps me aligned.

Day 191

Gratitude invites awareness of the present.

❧

I am fully here in this moment.
There is so much to appreciate.

Day 192

Gratitude is a quiet understanding.

❧

I understand my life more deeply.
Gratitude brings that awareness.

Day 193

Gratitude builds a sense of peace.

❧

Peace grows within me.
Gratitude nurtures that feeling.

Day 194

Gratitude invites emotional balance.

❧

I feel steady within myself.
Gratitude balances my emotions.

Day 195

Gratitude is a gentle shift in focus.

❧

I shift my attention to what is good.
Everything begins to feel different.

Day 196

Gratitude creates a sense of calm.

❧

I feel calm and relaxed.
Gratitude brings me into stillness.

DAY 197

Gratitude invites appreciation of the journey.

❧

I appreciate where I am in life.
Every step matters.

Day 198

Gratitude is a steady awareness.

❧

I stay aware of what I appreciate.
It shapes my experience.

Day 199

Gratitude invites deeper connection.

❧

I feel connected to my life and those around me.
Gratitude strengthens that bond.

Day 200

Gratitude marks meaningful progress.

❧

I recognize how far I have come.
I am grateful for my growth.

Day 201

Gratitude is a calm foundation.

I feel grounded and supported.
Gratitude is my foundation.

Day 202

Gratitude invites inner clarity.

❧

I understand myself more clearly.
Gratitude brings that insight.

Day 203

Gratitude creates a sense of ease.

I allow my life to feel easy.
Gratitude supports that flow.

Day 204

Gratitude is a gentle presence.

❧

I move through my day with quiet appreciation.
It stays with me.

Day 205

Gratitude invites peace of mind.

❧

My mind feels calm and relaxed.
Gratitude creates that peace.

Day 206

Gratitude is a steady influence.

Gratitude shapes how I experience my life.
It influences everything.

Day 207

Gratitude invites awareness of abundance.

❧

I see abundance everywhere.
There is always more than enough.

DAY 208

Gratitude creates emotional clarity.

❧

I understand my feelings more clearly.
Gratitude brings awareness.

DAY 209

Gratitude is a quiet strength within you.

I feel strong and steady.
Gratitude supports me.

Day 210

Gratitude invites harmony in your life.

I feel aligned and balanced.
Gratitude brings harmony.

Day 211

Gratitude is a peaceful awareness.

❧

I feel calm and present.
Gratitude keeps me centered.

Day 212

Gratitude invites a sense of enough.

❧

I feel content with what I have.
Nothing is missing.

Day 213

Gratitude creates a calm perspective.

&

I see my life with clarity and peace.
Gratitude shifts my view.

Day 214

Gratitude invites deeper appreciation.

I appreciate my life more fully.
There is always something to notice.

Day 215

Gratitude is a gentle flow of awareness.

I move through my day with appreciation.
It feels natural and steady.

Day 216

Gratitude invites presence in your life.

I stay present in what I am doing.
This moment matters.

Day 217

Gratitude creates a sense of connection.

❧

I feel connected to everything around me. Gratitude deepens that connection.

DAY 218

Gratitude invites inner calm.

❧

I feel calm within myself.
Gratitude brings me peace.

Day 219

Gratitude is a steady return.

No matter what happens, I return to appreciation.
It centers me.

Day 220

Gratitude is the path you walk.

❧

I move through life with appreciation and trust.
It guides me forward.

Day 221

Gratitude is a gentle awareness of what is good.

I notice what is working in my life.
There is always something to appreciate.

Day 222

Gratitude invites calm into your thoughts.

❧

My mind feels steady and clear.
Gratitude brings me peace.

Day 223

Gratitude is a quiet sense of trust.

❧

I trust where I am in my life.
Everything is unfolding as it should.

DAY 224

Gratitude creates a feeling of enough.

I feel content with what I have.
Nothing is missing in this moment.

Day 225

Gratitude is a steady presence within you.

❧

No matter what changes, gratitude remains.
It is always here for me.

Day 226

Gratitude invites a softer perspective.

❧

I see my life with kindness and understanding.
Everything feels lighter.

Day 227

Gratitude brings balance to your life.

&

I feel balanced and grounded.
Gratitude keeps me centered.

Day 228

Gratitude is a peaceful way of being.

&

I move through my day with calm appreciation. Peace follows me.

Day 229

Gratitude invites clarity in every moment.

❧

I see things more clearly.
Gratitude sharpens my awareness.

Day 230

Gratitude is a quiet strength.

❧

I feel strong and steady within myself.
Gratitude supports me.

Day 231

Gratitude creates a sense of flow.

❧

My life moves with ease.
Gratitude allows everything to flow naturally.

Day 232

Gratitude invites deeper connection to life.

❧

I feel connected to my experiences.
Gratitude deepens my awareness.

Day 233

Gratitude is a calm perspective.

&

I view my life with peace and clarity.
Everything feels more manageable.

Day 234

Gratitude creates emotional balance.

❧

I feel steady in my emotions.
Gratitude brings me back to center.

Day 235

Gratitude invites a sense of fulfillment.

I feel fulfilled in my life.
There is so much to appreciate.

Day 236

Gratitude is a steady guide within you.

❧

I trust my inner direction.
Gratitude keeps me aligned.

Day 237

Gratitude creates a quiet confidence.

I feel confident in my life.
Everything is unfolding in the right way.

Day 238

Gratitude invites awareness of abundance.

❧

I see abundance all around me.
There is always more than enough.

Day 239

Gratitude is a peaceful presence.

❧

I feel calm and present.
Gratitude keeps me grounded.

Day 240

Gratitude creates clarity in your life.

&

I understand my path more clearly.
Gratitude brings insight.

Day 241

Gratitude invites a sense of ease.

❧

I allow my life to feel easier.
Everything flows naturally.

Day 242

Gratitude is a gentle reminder of what matters.

I focus on what truly matters.
Everything else fades away.

Day 243

Gratitude creates a deeper awareness.

I see beyond the surface of my life.
There is more to appreciate.

Day 244

Gratitude invites calm energy.

❧

My energy feels peaceful and steady.
Gratitude supports that feeling.

Day 245

Gratitude is a steady connection.

I feel connected to myself and my life.
Gratitude strengthens that bond.

Day 246

Gratitude creates a sense of peace within.

&

I feel calm and at ease.
Gratitude brings me peace.

Day 247

Gratitude invites a sense of harmony.

❧

I feel aligned with my life.
Everything flows together.

DAY 248

Gratitude is a quiet awareness of joy.

❧

I notice moments of joy throughout my day.
They are always present.

Day 249

Gratitude creates a calm perspective.

❧

I see my life with clarity and peace.
Gratitude shifts my view.

Day 250

Gratitude marks meaningful growth.

❧

I recognize how far I have come.
I am grateful for my progress.

Day 251

Gratitude invites a steady mindset.

❧

My thoughts feel calm and focused.
Gratitude supports my clarity.

Day 252

Gratitude is a gentle presence in your life.

❧

I move through my day with quiet appreciation.
It stays with me.

Day 253

Gratitude creates awareness of what is working.

I focus on what is going well.
There is always something to appreciate.

Day 254

Gratitude invites emotional clarity.

❧

I understand my feelings more clearly.
Gratitude brings awareness.

Day 255

Gratitude is a peaceful state of being.

I feel calm and at ease within myself.
Gratitude brings me peace.

Day 256

Gratitude creates a sense of flow in your life.

&

My life flows with ease.
Gratitude keeps me aligned.

Day 257

Gratitude invites deeper presence.

I stay present in each moment.
There is so much to appreciate.

Day 258

Gratitude is a steady awareness of the good.

❧

I notice what is good in my life.
It continues to grow.

Day 259

Gratitude creates balance within you.

I feel balanced and grounded.
Gratitude centers me.

Day 260

Gratitude invites a sense of peace.

❧

I feel peaceful within myself.
Gratitude supports that feeling.

Day 261

Gratitude is a quiet source of strength.

I feel strong and steady.
Gratitude supports me from within.

Day 262

Gratitude creates a calm awareness.

I move through my day with quiet appreciation.
Everything feels more peaceful.

Day 263

Gratitude invites a sense of clarity.

❧

I see my life more clearly.
Gratitude brings understanding.

Day 264

Gratitude is a gentle shift in perspective.

❧

I shift my focus to what is good.
Everything begins to feel different.

Day 265

Gratitude creates a sense of fulfillment.

I feel fulfilled in my life.
There is always something to appreciate.

Day 266

Gratitude invites a steady flow of energy.

❧

My energy feels balanced and calm.
Gratitude supports my flow.

Day 267

Gratitude is a peaceful awareness of life.

I feel calm and present.
Gratitude keeps me centered.

DAY 268

Gratitude creates a sense of connection.

❧

I feel connected to everything around me.
Gratitude deepens that connection.

Day 269

Gratitude invites a sense of ease.

❧

I allow my life to feel easier.
Everything flows naturally.

DAY 270

Gratitude is a steady return to what matters.

❧

I come back to what matters most.
Gratitude keeps me focused.

Day 271

Gratitude creates a calm and steady mind.

❧

My mind feels quiet and clear.
Gratitude brings peace.

Day 272

Gratitude invites awareness of the present.

❧

I am fully here in this moment.
There is so much to appreciate.

Day 273

Gratitude is a gentle reminder of enough.

ࡂ

I have enough.
I am enough.
This moment is enough.

Day 274

Gratitude creates a sense of harmony.

I feel aligned with my life.
Everything flows together.

Day 275

Gratitude invites a peaceful perspective.

❧

I see my life with calm and clarity.
Everything feels more manageable.

Day 276

Gratitude is a steady awareness of abundance.

❧

I see abundance in my life.
There is always more than enough.

Day 277

Gratitude creates emotional balance.

I feel steady within myself.
Gratitude supports my emotions.

Day 278

Gratitude invites deeper appreciation.

❧

I appreciate my life more fully.
There is always something to notice.

DAY 279

Gratitude is a calm and steady presence.

I feel grounded and supported.
Gratitude keeps me centered.

Day 280

Gratitude creates a sense of peace.

❧

I feel calm and at ease.
Gratitude brings me peace.

Day 281

Gratitude invites clarity and focus.

I see my path clearly.
Gratitude brings direction.

Day 282

Gratitude is a gentle awareness of the good.

❧

I notice what is good in my life.
It continues to grow.

Day 283

Gratitude creates a steady mindset.

❧

My thoughts feel calm and balanced.
Gratitude supports my clarity.

DAY 284

Gratitude invites presence in your life.

❧

I stay present in each moment.
This moment matters.

Day 285

Gratitude is a quiet sense of trust.

❧

I trust where I am in life.
Everything is unfolding for me.

Day 286

Gratitude creates a sense of flow.

❧

My life flows naturally.
Gratitude keeps me aligned.

Day 287

Gratitude invites a calm awareness.

I feel calm and present.
Gratitude keeps me centered.

Day 288

Gratitude is a steady connection to life.

I feel connected to my life and purpose. Gratitude strengthens that connection.

Day 289

Gratitude creates a peaceful perspective.

❧

I see my life with clarity and calm.
Everything feels more manageable.

Day 290

Gratitude invites emotional ease.

❧

I feel relaxed within myself.
Gratitude softens my experience.

Day 291

Gratitude is a gentle return to presence.

❧

I come back to this moment.
There is so much to appreciate.

Day 292

Gratitude creates a sense of balance.

I feel balanced and grounded.
Gratitude centers me.

Day 293

Gratitude invites a deeper awareness.

I see beyond the surface.
There is more to appreciate.

Day 294

Gratitude is a steady source of peace.

❧

I feel calm within myself.
Gratitude brings me peace.

Day 295

Gratitude creates a sense of fulfillment.

I feel fulfilled in my life.
There is always something to appreciate.

Day 296

Gratitude invites clarity in your life.

❧

I see my life more clearly.
Gratitude brings understanding.

Day 297

Gratitude is a gentle awareness of what is.

I accept my life as it is.
Gratitude helps me appreciate it fully.

Day 298

Gratitude creates a calm and steady energy.

My energy feels peaceful and balanced.
Gratitude supports my flow.

DAY 299

Gratitude invites a sense of peace within.

❧

I feel calm and at ease.
Gratitude brings me peace.

Day 300

Gratitude is a beautiful way to live.

❧

I choose to live with appreciation.
It transforms my life.

Day 301

Gratitude is a calm awareness of life.

I feel present and aware.
There is so much to appreciate.

Day 302

Gratitude invites peace into your mind.

My thoughts feel calm and steady.
Gratitude brings me clarity.

Day 303

Gratitude is a gentle connection to the present.

I stay connected to this moment.
It holds everything I need.

Day 304

Gratitude creates a sense of ease.

❧

I allow my life to feel easier.
Everything flows naturally.

Day 305

Gratitude invites a steady perspective.

I see my life with calm and clarity.
Everything feels more manageable.

Day 306

Gratitude is a quiet source of strength.

❧

I feel strong and supported.
Gratitude steadies me.

Day 307

Gratitude creates awareness of the good.

❧

I notice what is working in my life.
It continues to grow.

Day 308

Gratitude invites a sense of balance.

❧

I feel grounded and centered.
Gratitude keeps me aligned.

DAY 309

Gratitude is a steady presence.

No matter what changes, gratitude remains.
It is always here for me.

Day 310

Gratitude creates a calm energy.

❧

My energy feels peaceful and steady.
Gratitude supports my flow.

DAY 311

Gratitude invites clarity in your life.

❧

I see my path more clearly.
Gratitude brings direction.

Day 312

Gratitude is a gentle reminder of enough.

❧

I have enough.
I am enough.
This moment is enough.

Day 313

Gratitude creates a sense of peace.

❧

I feel calm and at ease.
Gratitude brings me peace.

Day 314

Gratitude invites deeper awareness.

I see beyond the surface of my life.
There is always more to appreciate.

Day 315

Gratitude is a steady return to presence.

❧

I come back to this moment.
It is enough.

Day 316

Gratitude creates a sense of fulfillment.

❧

I feel fulfilled in my life.
There is always something to appreciate.

Day 317

Gratitude invites emotional balance.

❧

I feel steady within myself.
Gratitude supports my emotions.

Day 318

Gratitude is a calm and steady awareness.

❧

I move through my day with quiet appreciation. Everything feels more peaceful.

Day 319

Gratitude creates a sense of connection.

&

I feel connected to my life and those around me. Gratitude deepens that connection.

Day 320

Gratitude invites a sense of harmony.

❧

I feel aligned with my life.
Everything flows together.

Day 321

Gratitude is a quiet understanding.

🙞

I understand my life more clearly.
Gratitude brings insight.

Day 322

Gratitude creates a steady mindset.

❧

My thoughts feel calm and balanced.
Gratitude supports my clarity.

Day 323

Gratitude invites presence in your life.

I stay present in each moment.
This moment matters.

DAY 324

Gratitude is a gentle awareness of what is.

❧

I accept my life as it is.
Gratitude helps me appreciate it fully.

Day 325

Gratitude creates a sense of flow.

❧

My life flows naturally.
Gratitude keeps me aligned.

Day 326

Gratitude invites calm energy.

My energy feels peaceful and steady.
Gratitude supports my flow.

Day 327

Gratitude is a steady source of peace.

&

I feel calm within myself.
Gratitude brings me peace.

DAY 328

Gratitude creates clarity in your life.

I see my life more clearly.
Gratitude brings understanding.

Day 329

Gratitude invites a sense of ease.

❧

I allow my life to feel easier.
Everything flows naturally.

Day 330

Gratitude is a quiet confidence.

I trust where I am in my life.
Everything is unfolding for me.

Day 331

Gratitude creates a sense of balance.

I feel balanced and grounded.
Gratitude centers me.

DAY 332

Gratitude invites awareness of abundance.

I see abundance everywhere.
There is always more than enough.

Day 333

Gratitude is a gentle reminder of the present.

I return to this moment.
There is so much to appreciate.

Day 334

Gratitude creates a peaceful perspective.

&

I see my life with calm and clarity.
Everything feels more manageable.

Day 335

Gratitude invites deeper appreciation.

❧

I appreciate my life more fully.
There is always something to notice.

Day 336

Gratitude is a steady awareness of the good.

❧

I notice what is good in my life.
It continues to grow.

Day 337

Gratitude creates emotional ease.

I feel relaxed within myself.
Gratitude softens my experience.

Day 338

Gratitude invites a calm awareness.

❧

I feel calm and present.
Gratitude keeps me centered.

Day 339

Gratitude is a quiet connection to life.

I feel connected to everything around me. Gratitude deepens that connection.

Day 340

Gratitude creates a sense of peace within.

❧

I feel calm and at ease.
Gratitude brings me peace.

Day 341

Gratitude invites clarity and focus.

☙

I see my path clearly.
Gratitude brings direction.

Day 342

Gratitude is a gentle presence.

❧

I move through my day with quiet appreciation.
It stays with me.

Day 343

Gratitude creates a sense of fulfillment.

&

I feel fulfilled in my life.
There is always something to appreciate.

Day 344

Gratitude invites a sense of harmony.

&

I feel aligned with my life.
Everything flows together.

Day 345

Gratitude is a steady return to peace.

No matter what happens, I return to appreciation.
It centers me.

Day 346

Gratitude creates a calm and steady mind.

&

My mind feels quiet and clear.
Gratitude brings peace.

Day 347

Gratitude invites awareness of the present.

❧

I am fully here in this moment.
There is so much to appreciate.

DAY 348

Gratitude is a gentle awareness of enough.

❧

I have enough.
I am enough.
This moment is enough.

Day 349

Gratitude creates a peaceful state of being.

I feel calm and at ease within myself.
Gratitude brings me peace.

Day 350

Gratitude invites a deeper connection.

❧

I feel connected to my life and purpose.
Gratitude strengthens that connection.

Day 351

Gratitude is a steady awareness of life.

I notice what is good in my life.
It continues to grow.

Day 352

Gratitude creates a sense of balance.

&

I feel balanced and grounded.
Gratitude centers me.

Day 353

Gratitude invites calm thinking.

❧

My thoughts feel peaceful and clear.
Gratitude brings me clarity.

Day 354

Gratitude is a quiet strength.

❧

I feel strong and supported.
Gratitude steadies me.

Day 355

Gratitude creates a sense of flow.

My life flows naturally.
Gratitude keeps me aligned.

Day 356

Gratitude invites a sense of peace.

I feel calm and at ease.
Gratitude brings me peace.

Day 357

Gratitude is a gentle return to the present.

I come back to this moment.
It is enough.

Day 358

Gratitude creates awareness of abundance.

❧

I see abundance everywhere.
There is always more than enough.

DAY 359

Gratitude invites emotional ease.

I feel relaxed within myself.
Gratitude softens my experience.

Day 360

Gratitude is a steady source of calm.

❧

I feel calm and centered.
Gratitude supports me.

Day 361

Gratitude creates a peaceful perspective.

I see my life with clarity and calm.
Everything feels more manageable.

Day 362

Gratitude invites deeper appreciation.

❧

I appreciate my life more fully.
There is always something to notice.

Day 363

Gratitude is a quiet awareness of the good.

I notice what is good in my life.
It continues to grow.

Day 364

Gratitude creates a sense of fulfillment.

❧

I feel fulfilled in my life.
There is always something to appreciate.

Day 365

Gratitude is the way you live your life.

I live with appreciation, trust, and presence.
My life reflects that choice

A Final Thought

Gratitude is not about pretending life is perfect.

It is about learning to notice the beauty that exists within it.

May these pages continue to remind you:

there is always something to hold onto,

something to appreciate,

something to begin again for.

And most importantly,

may you never forget how much beauty already exists within you.

Acknowledgement

Some friendships are gifts.
Tracy, ours has been one of the greatest blessings of my life.

For more than forty years, you have been a constant light. A steady reminder that joy is a choice, gratitude is a practice, and positivity is a way of living. You have always protected the energy around you so beautifully. If a conversation turns dark or negative, you gently guide it back toward the light, toward hope, toward something better. That is such a rare gift.

You have taught me, simply by being yourself, that life feels lighter when we choose love, laughter, kindness, and gratitude over fear and negativity.

Every single conversation with you leaves me feeling happier, calmer, and more grounded. You are truly one of the most positive souls I have ever known, and I am endlessly grateful for your friendship, your heart, your wisdom, and your presence in my life.

Thank you for the forty-plus years of friendship, encouragement, laughter, and light.

Love always,
Christine

About the Author

&

Christine Zanjanipour is the author of *The Manifest Principles* and a passionate advocate for intentional living, gratitude, and personal transformation.

Through her writing, speaking, and daily practices, she encourages others to slow down, reconnect with themselves, and create a life rooted in clarity, presence, and possibility.

She lives in the mountains of Colorado, where much of her inspiration comes from nature, stillness, and the beauty found in everyday moments.

Gratitude changes everything.

www.ingramcontent.com/pod-product-compliance
Lightning Source LLC
LaVergne TN
LVHW010632110826
845149LV00014B/2833
* 9 7 9 8 9 9 3 9 0 1 3 9 8 *